How to Analyze the Films of

JAMES
CAMERON

by Susan E. Hamen

ABDO
Publishing Company

Essential Critiques

How to Analyze the Films of

JAMES
CAMERON

by Susan E. Hamen

Content Consultant: Michele Schreiber, PhD
assistant professor, Department of Film Studies
Emory University

Credits

Published by ABDO Publishing Company, 8000 West 78th Street, Edina, Minnesota 55439. Copyright © 2012 by Abdo Consulting Group, Inc. International copyrights reserved in all countries. No part of this book may be reproduced in any form without written permission from the publisher. The Essential Library™ is a trademark and logo of ABDO Publishing Company.

Printed in the United States of America,
North Mankato, Minnesota
062011
092011

 THIS BOOK CONTAINS AT LEAST 10% RECYCLED MATERIALS.

Editor: Mari Kesselring
Copy Editor: Sarah Beckman
Interior Design and Production: Christa Schneider
Cover Design: Marie Tupy

Library of Congress Cataloging-in-Publication Data
Hamen, Susan E.
  How to analyze the films of James Cameron / by Susan E. Hamen.
      p. cm. -- (Essential critiques)
  Includes bibliographical references.
  ISBN 978-1-61783-088-4
  1. Cameron, James, 1954---Criticism and interpretation--Juvenile literature. 2. Film criticism--Juvenile literature. I. Title.
  PN1998.3.C352H35 2011
  791.43023'3092--dc22
                                        2011006298

Table of Contents

1

Introduction to Critiques

What Is Critical Theory?

What do you usually do as a member of an audience watching a movie? You probably enjoy the settings, the costumes, and the sound track. You learn about the characters as they are developed through dialogue and other interactions. You might be drawn in by the plot of the movie, eager to find out what happens next. Yet these are only a few of many ways of understanding and appreciating a movie. What if you are interested in delving more deeply? You might want to learn more about the director and how his or her personal background is reflected in the film. Or you might want to examine what the film says about society—how it depicts the roles of women and minorities, for example. If so, you have entered the realm of critical theory.

Critical theory helps you learn how various works of art, literature, music, theater, film, and other endeavors either support or challenge the way society behaves. Critical theory is the evaluation and interpretation of a work using different philosophies, or schools of thought. Critical theory can be used to understand all types of cultural productions.

There are many different critical theories. If you are analyzing a movie, each theory asks you to look at the work from a different perspective. Some theories address social issues, while others focus on the director's life, what role the direction plays in the overall film, or the time period in which the film was written or set. For example, the critical theory that asks how a director's life affected the work is called biographical criticism. Other common, broad schools of criticism include historical criticism, feminist criticism, auteur criticism, and ideological criticism.

What Is the Purpose of Critical Theory?

Critical theory can open your mind to new ways of thinking. It can help you evaluate a movie from a new perspective, directing your attention to issues and messages you may not otherwise recognize in a work. For example, applying feminist criticism to a film may make you aware of female stereotypes perpetuated in the work. Applying a critical theory to a work helps you learn about the person who created it or the society that enjoyed it. You can explore how the movie is perceived by current cultures.

How Do You Apply Critical Theory?

You conduct a critique when you use a critical theory to examine and question a work. The theory you choose is a lens through which you can view the work, or a springboard for asking questions about the work. Applying a critical theory helps you to think critically about the work. You are free to question the work and make an assertion about it. If you choose to examine a film using biographical criticism, for example, you want to know how the director's personal background inspired or shaped the work. You could explore why the director was drawn to the story. For instance, are there any parallels between a particular character's life and the director's life?

Forming a Thesis

Ask your question and find answers in the work or other related materials. Then you can create a thesis. The thesis is the key point in your critique. It is your argument about the work based on the tenets, or beliefs, of the theory you are using. For example, if you are using biographical criticism to ask how the director's life inspired the work, your thesis could be worded as follows: Director Teng Xiong, raised in refugee camps in Southeast Asia, drew upon her experiences to direct the movie *No Home for Me*.

> **How to Make a Thesis Statement**
>
> In a critique, a thesis statement typically appears at the end of the introductory paragraph. It is usually only one sentence long and states the author's main idea.

Providing Evidence

Once you have formed a thesis, you must provide evidence to support it. Evidence might take the form of examples and quotations from the work itself—such as dialogue from a film. Articles about the movie or personal interviews with the director might also support your ideas. You may wish to address what other critics have written about the work. Quotes from these individuals may help support your claim. If you find any quotes or examples that contradict your thesis, you will need to create an argument against them.

For instance: <u>Many critics have pointed to the heroine of *No Home for Me* as a powerless victim of circumstances. However, through her dialogue and strong actions, she is clearly depicted as someone who seeks to shape her own future.</u>

How to Support a Thesis Statement

A critique should include several arguments. Arguments support a thesis claim. An argument is one or two sentences long and is supported by evidence from the work being discussed.

Organize the arguments into paragraphs. These paragraphs make up the body of the critique.

In This Book

In this book, you will read overviews of famous movies by director James Cameron, each followed by a critique. Each critique will use one theory and apply it to one work. Critical thinking sections will give you a chance to consider other theses and questions about the work. Did you agree with the author's application of the theory? What other questions are raised by the thesis and its arguments? You can also find out what other critics think about each particular film. Then, in the You Critique It section in the final pages of this book, you will have an opportunity to create your own critique.

Look for the Guides

Throughout the chapters that analyze the works, thesis statements have been highlighted. The box next to the thesis helps explain what questions are being raised about the work. Supporting arguments have been underlined. The boxes next to the arguments help explain how these points support the thesis. Look for these guides throughout each critique.

Cameron holds three Oscars he received for *Titanic*.

2

A Closer Look at James Cameron

Few moviemakers ever obtain the level of distinction that James Cameron has reached. Renowned for being king of the science-fiction movie genre and famous for his blockbuster productions, Cameron has risen to be a highly sought-after screenwriter and director in Hollywood today.

The Young Canadian

On August 16, 1954, James Cameron was born to Philip and Shirley Cameron of Kapuskasing, a town in northern Ontario, Canada. When James was five, the family moved to Chippawa near Niagara Falls. James was a very bright boy. In elementary school, he was moved forward two full grades. He was a voracious reader, and was also interested in

French oceanographer Jacques Cousteau's television documentaries, which introduced him to the foreign world of life under the sea.

Bitten by the Movie Bug

In 1968, when James was 14, he saw Stanley Kubrick's movie *2001: A Space Odyssey*. In that moment, James decided he wanted his future to be in creating special effects. James and a friend became obsessed with shooting footage on a Super 8 camera. Their amateur films included model spaceships they had built that engaged in intergalactic wars. "It's all garbage," James says about his first films.[1] However, the films helped him improve his skills.

Off to Hollywood

At the age of 16, James's father received a job transfer to Orange County, California. "Jim said, 'Can we leave tomorrow?' He knew he was getting close to Hollywood," his father remembered.[2] James enrolled in Fullerton College with plans to major in physics, but he switched his major to English before dropping out of college altogether. He met some fellow students who were also interested in science fiction. He began reading screenplays and writing in his spare time, while making money working as a janitor and a truck driver.

In the Movie Business

In 1977, *Star Wars* hit the big screen. It was the inspiration Cameron needed to pursue his own dreams of making a special-effects movie. He and fellow film enthusiast Bill Wisher secured enough funding to produce a 12-minute film entitled *Xenogenesis*. The film would serve as a persuasive demonstration of Cameron's ability behind the camera and with special effects.

The next year, Cameron was hired at Roger Corman's New World Pictures studio as a miniature model builder. Within months, Cameron became the art director of the film *Battle Beyond the Stars* (1980). His special-effects techniques were impressive, and Cameron continued to hone his craft. Meanwhile, Cameron married Sharon Williams on February 14, 1978. However, their marriage ended by 1984.

In 1981, Cameron earned his first chance at directing a film with *Piranha II: The Spawning*. The project was a disaster. Others involved in producing the film kept Cameron from directing it the way he had hoped. However, during the process, a frustrated, exhausted Cameron had a nightmare about a robot traveling back in time to kill him. It was this idea that Cameron would develop into *The Terminator,* the film that would catapult his career.

While Cameron earned money writing the screenplays for *Rambo: First Blood Part II,* which starred Sylvester Stallone, and *Aliens,* the follow-up to Ridley Scott's 1979 film *Alien,* he completed his screenplay for *The Terminator. The Terminator* opened at number one at the box office during its opening weekend in 1984 and made $78 million worldwide. The project also brought Cameron together with his second wife, producer of the film, Gale Ann Hurd.

More Successes

Following the success of *The Terminator,* Cameron was hired to direct *Aliens.* Released in 1986, the film pulled in $130 million worldwide. *Aliens* won Academy Awards for best visual effects and best sound effects. Soon, everyone in Hollywood wanted to meet the successful young director who was unquestionably brilliant, yet was earning a reputation for being difficult to work with. At age 32, Cameron was a perfectionist when it came to his films. He was already focusing his energy on his next vision, an underwater special-effects adventure titled *The Abyss* (1989).

In 1991, Cameron furthered his success with *Terminator 2: Judgment Day.* The film raked in a whopping $500 million. In the aftermath of his success with *Terminator 2,* Cameron formed Lightstorm Entertainment, his very own production company. He also divorced his third wife, Kathryn Bigelow, and married the movie's heroine, Linda Hamilton. The couple had a daughter, Josephine Archer, in 1993.

In December 1997, Cameron's *Titanic* left audiences spellbound. Far exceeding the projected budget, the film cost $200 million to produce. In its first weekend, *Titanic* grossed more than $25.5 million and went on to make history, grossing more than $1 billion worldwide and making it the top-grossing film of all time. The film took home 11 Oscars, including best picture and best director.

Between 2000 and 2009, Cameron produced, wrote, or directed various projects, including the television series *Dark Angel* and *Terminator: The*

Sarah Connor Chronicles and the underwater documentaries *Ghosts of the Abyss* (2003) and *Aliens of the Deep* (2005). He also became more involved with exploration, partaking in 41 deep-submersible dives to explore the bioluminescent flora and fauna beneath the ocean's surface.

Cameron and Hamilton had divorced in 1999, and six months later, Cameron married actress Suzy Amis, who had starred in *Titanic.* The couple had twins Claire and Quinn in April 2001 and another daughter, Elizabeth Rose, in 2006.

In 2009, Cameron was back to breaking records, this time his own. Cameron's film *Avatar,* the long-anticipated science-fiction extravaganza, opened at the box office in December to critical acclaim and commercial success. Although production costs topped an estimated $310 million, the film smashed box office records and would go on to be the first film to gross more than $2 billion worldwide. Cameron broke his own record, replacing *Titanic*'s record for highest-grossing film of all time with *Avatar*. The stereoscopic filmmaking Cameron employed for *Avatar* was a breakthrough in cinematic technology.

The Future

Cameron has become a renowned filmmaker and master of the science-fiction genre. He is a perfectionist and possesses the vision to push the boundaries of film, special effects, and cinematic technology. After the release of *Avatar,* he began working on two sequels, the first one scheduled for theatrical release in 2014 and the third installment slated for 2015. No one knows what he will dream up next.

Cameron and his wife, Suzy Amis, at the 2010 Academy Awards

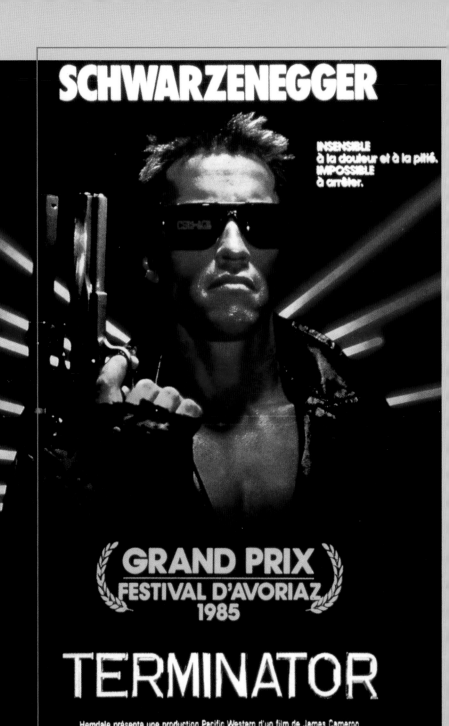

The Terminator starred Arnold Schwarzenegger.

3

An Overview of
The Terminator

The Terminator opens on a bleak, futuristic
Los Angeles in the year 2029. A defense-network
computer called Skynet has orchestrated a nuclear
war. Humans have been rounded up and disposed
of by human-looking robots called Terminators.
Civilization lies in destruction, and a group of
human resistance fighters battle to stay alive. A
scroll of text appears, explaining to the viewer:

> *The machines rose from the ashes of the*
> *nuclear fire. Their war to exterminate*
> *mankind had raged for decades, but the*
> *final battle would not be fought in the future.*
> *It would be fought here, in our present.*
> *Tonight . . .*[1]

The scene then cuts to Los Angeles in the year
1984, time: 1:52 a.m. A garbage truck loses power

amid a storm of flashing blue electric currents. As the smoke clears, a naked Terminator is seen crouched on the ground. He approaches three street punks and demands their clothing.

The scene cuts to an alleyway where another man falls to the ground from a riot of flashing blue lightning. Also naked, he takes the pants of a homeless man in the alley as the police stop, see what is happening, and then give chase. The man, who later identifies himself as Kyle Reese, overpowers one of the officers and takes his gun. He demands to know the current day and year, but a squad car pulls up before the officer can tell him anything more than that it is May 12.

Kyle escapes the police, steals clothes from a store, and finds a phone booth. He locates the name "Sarah Connor" in the phone book—of which there are three listings—rips the page out and takes off. It is later revealed that John Connor is the fearless leader of the resistance, and in an effort to crush the resistance, the Terminator has been sent back in time to kill John's mother, destroying any chance of John Connor ever being born. Kyle is the resistance fighter who volunteers to follow him into the past to protect Sarah.

While the hunted Sarah Connor is working at a diner, the Terminator enters an Alamo Sport Shop. He arms himself with a 12-gauge shotgun, a .45 Longslide with laser sighting, and a 9mm Uzi. He then shoots the shopkeeper. The Terminator then makes his own stop at a phone booth to secure the addresses of all potential Sarah Connors. He drives a stolen station wagon to the residence of the first Sarah and kills her.

Meanwhile, Kyle hotwires a car at a construction site. This prompts a flashback to his own time, the year 2029. He relives the destruction, devastation, and dire circumstances of mankind in the year 2029. He and his fellow soldiers fight an ardent battle against Skynet and its army of high-tech machines.

Sarah Connor

Meanwhile, Sarah and her roommate Ginger prepare for a night out, until Sarah's date cancels. Sarah decides to go to a movie alone, leaving Ginger and her boyfriend, Matt, at the apartment. Kyle has been watching her apartment and follows her. Unbeknownst to Sarah, Lieutenant Ed Traxler and Detective Hal Vukovich are trying to reach her in order to protect her, too. Alone at a bar, she eats pizza and hears on the television news that two Sarah Connors have been murdered. She rushes to a pay phone, where she discovers in the phone book that she is the next listed Sarah Connor. She attempts to make a call, but the phone is out of order. Leaving the bar, she notices Kyle following her and ducks into a nightclub. Her attempt at dialing 911 is met with a busy signal.

In the following scene, the Terminator enters Sarah's apartment, killing Matt and then Ginger, assuming she is Sarah. However, as Ginger lies dying on the floor, the phone rings. The machine picks up the call and the Terminator hears, "Ginger, this is Sarah! Pick up if you're there!"[2] She then reveals her location to Ginger, asking for help.

Shortly thereafter, the Terminator enters the nightclub, but Kyle helps Sarah escape, driving her away at top speed in a stolen vehicle. Terrified, Sarah is unsure if she can trust Kyle, who tells her he is a sergeant who has been assigned to protect her. "You've been targeted for termination," he tells her.[3] He then explains to her that he and the Terminator are from the future and that her enemy is a Cyberdyne Systems Model 101 cyborg, which is constructed of a hyperalloy combat chassis, is microprocessor controlled, and is covered with real living human skin and hair to look human. It is emotionless and has one objective. It will not stop until she is dead.

As the two hide in a parking garage, Kyle tells Sarah about the future. He grew up after the war in the ruins, hiding from hunter-killers, or H-Ks, that were built to round up humans for disposal. He explains that one man taught them to fight—John Connor, her future son.

The Terminator discovers the two. Another chase scene ensues and ends in a crash. Kyle and Sarah are surrounded by the police, but the Terminator has escaped. At the police station, the lieutenant, the detective, and a criminal psychologist assure Sarah that Kyle is crazy. However, when the Terminator breaks into the police station, killing countless officers, Kyle is the only one who can save Sarah.

Kyle and Sarah escape the Terminator in a stolen car. However, Kyle is shot in the process. Sarah tries to clean the wound for him as the two are hiding in a culvert after they run out of gas. There, Sarah asks Kyle to describe her future son John. Kyle tells her he is strong and trusted. His father died before the war, but Sarah would be the one to teach her son to fight and organize the resistance. "I can't even balance my checkbook. . . . I didn't ask for this honor, and I don't want it," Sarah scoffs.[4] Kyle then gives her a message from her son in which John tells her to be strong and to survive.

The next day, they make it to a motel. Kyle heads out for supplies, and Sarah showers and then calls her mother, who asks where she is. Sarah reveals their location, and the scene cuts to the Terminator at her mother's house, who is impersonating her mother's voice on the phone. He has killed her mother.

When Kyle returns, he shows her how to make homemade bombs. Later that night, Kyle admits to Sarah that John had given him a picture of Sarah and that he had fallen in love with her. She, too, has fallen for Kyle, and the two have sex.

The Final Battle

Afterward, a dog outside barks, and Kyle realizes the Terminator has found them. They escape by stealing a pickup truck. During the chase, the pickup truck Kyle and Sarah are in flips, injuring Kyle. The Terminator is caught in a gasoline-tank truck explosion. Sarah, initially believing the Terminator is destroyed, is shocked to see the robotic skeleton coming toward her.

Sarah helps Kyle flee into a factory. A weakened Kyle jams one of the pipe bombs he helped Sarah make into the torso of the Terminator. It explodes, leaving the Terminator without legs and one arm. Kyle is killed in the process, and Sarah is left with injuries to her leg. What is left of the Terminator springs to life and drags its way toward Sarah. She lures it onto a conveyor belt of a hydraulic press and crushes it in the machinery, destroying the Terminator.

In the final scene of the film, Sarah drives a Jeep through Mexico. She is pregnant. Kyle is the father of her future son John. On her drive, she records audiotapes for John. She briefly explains, "If you don't send Kyle, you can never be."[5] She stops for gas, and a young boy snaps an instant Kodamatic picture of her. It is the picture that John gives Kyle in the future.

Kyle Reese, *left*, is sent from the future to protect Sarah Connor, *right*.

4

How to Apply Historical Criticism to *The Terminator*

What Is Historical Criticism?

Some forms of criticism draw from external concepts to help analyze the work's meaning. Historical criticism is an example of this and can be applied to a book, a film, a theater production, or a piece of art or music. A historical critique first looks at the historical and social circumstances of the time in which the work was created. It then analyzes how the work was influenced by historical occurrences and social surroundings during the time it was produced.

Applying Historical Criticism to *The Terminator*

In the 1980s, the United States was experiencing the beginning of massive computer-technology growth, facilitated by the creation of Microsoft and Apple in the late 1970s, and the emergence of semiconductor production in Silicon Valley, California. Although computers were not new in 1980, personal use of computers was in its infancy. A 1982 *National Geographic* article suggested:

> *Befriending the computer, and putting it to work and play in daily life a decade before most of us found the courage to touch a keyboard, Silicon Valley and its families may well be a glimpse of a computer-and-communications culture that is the prototype of the future.[1]*

But along with the growth of the computer industry and society's increased reliance upon technology, came a feeling of dread. Many wondered if society was becoming too dependent on technology. Were we setting ourselves up for a catastrophic downfall? It is not surprising that these insecurities about technology show up in films of the time. The film *The Terminator*, which was released in 1984, mirrors the wariness of

Thesis Statement

Here, the author introduces the thesis statement: "The film *The Terminator*, which was released in 1984, mirrors the wariness of US society at the dawn of the computer age of the advance of technology and the fear of how it would affect humanity."

US society at the dawn of the computer age of the advance of technology and the fear of how it would affect humanity.

The Terminator predicts that the destruction of humanity happens via humanity's own creation—technology. As the movie opens, the audience learns that in the future, a defense-network computer has become so advanced, it evolves into a form of intelligence that surpasses human intelligence and orchestrates a new holocaust at the hands of machines. This results in the near extinction of the entire human race.

Throughout the film, machines are able to defeat and overcome humans. As author and professor Jay David Bolter argued at the time of *The Terminator*'s release,

> *Many ages in the past have shown great promise while facing great difficulties, yet our age is perhaps unique in that its problems and its promise come from*

Argument One

The author begins with the first argument: "*The Terminator* predicts that the destruction of humanity happens via humanity's own creation—technology."

Argument Two

The author continues, offering another argument that reflects how technology in the film adversely affects humans: "Throughout the film, machines are able to defeat and overcome humans."

The Terminator lacks a sense of humanity.

the same source, from the extraordinary achievements of science and technology.[2]

The Terminator breaks into Sarah's apartment and kills her roommate, assuming Ginger is Sarah. Ginger does not hear him break in because she is in the kitchen, ears covered by her Walkman headphones, music blaring. Ginger's use of a technological device—the Walkman—makes her less able to defend herself against the Terminator and leads to her death. As Ginger lies dying on the floor, Sarah calls the apartment to ask Ginger for help. The answering machine picks up the call, and the Terminator hears a frantic Sarah leave the message and give her location. While the answering machine may be a helpful tool to communicate, had it not been for the message, the Terminator would have left thinking its work was done, instead of continuing its pursuit of Sarah.

Through the representation of the Terminator, a machine, the film depicts technology as dangerous because it has a complete lack of emotion, conscience, and sense of humanity. The Terminator, a walking and talking representation of technology, kills two Sarah Connors, Ginger, Matt, and a myriad of other victims before it zeroes in on the real Sarah Connor. It will mindlessly kill anyone who stands in the way of its mission, or in order to get to information leading to Sarah Connor. As Kyle Reese explains to Sarah, "It can't be bargained with. It can't be reasoned with. It doesn't feel pity or remorse or fear. And it absolutely will not stop ever! Until you are dead."[3]

> **Argument Three**
> The author next argues the point that computers have no human attributes and do not have the ability to reason, feel, or factor in human ethics and morality.

Argument Four

The author continues with the argument that: "humans in the film are still depicted as superior beings to the Terminator and technology because of their humanity."

<u>Although flawed and vulnerable, humans in the film are still depicted as superior beings to the Terminator and technology because of their humanity.</u> On the run, trying to elude the Terminator, Sarah and Kyle fall in love. It is that emotion and human connection that leads to the conception of humanity's future hope, John Connor. By the end of the film, Kyle is willing to die to protect Sarah, and, while sacrificing himself, he significantly damages the Terminator.

Conclusion

The final paragraph concludes the author's critique and sums up the arguments that support the assertion of the thesis.

The Terminator debuted at a time when technology was beginning to affect everyday life. In a world that was evolving to rely more and more on computers, people began questioning how far humanity's dependence would go and when the backlash would occur. *The Terminator* portrays the collective concerns of this technological dependence of the early 1980s and proposes the course of human fate the more advanced technologies become.

Thinking Critically about *The Terminator*

Now it is your turn to assess the critique. Consider these questions:

1. The author argues that the film reveals an anxiety about technology that was present in the 1980s. Do you agree with the author's thesis? Why or why not?

2. Do you think the film shows technology in mostly a negative light as the author suggests? Are there any examples of technology being used in a positive way?

3. Do the anxieties about technology apparent in *The Terminator* still exist in society today? Are these anxieties showcased in any recent films?

Other Approaches

The critique you have read is just one way to approach *The Terminator* through the lens of historical criticism. What are some other ways to apply this approach to the film? Following are two different ways to apply historical criticism to *The Terminator*.

A New Female Hero

Within the science-fiction genre, *The Terminator* was one of the first movies to portray a heroine capable of defeating an otherworldly being. In the 1980s, female movie characters more often deferred to the male for the role of hero and protector. Many second-wave feminists were still fighting for equality for women in laws and culture in the early 1980s. The film reflects this notion.

Such a critique might have the thesis statement: *The Terminator* serves as a historical example of the second-wave feminist struggle to shift from the female character portrayed as a damsel in distress to that of a capable woman.

A Glimpse into the Future: Bleak

The future world that *The Terminator* suggests is a mass of destruction. Buildings lie in ruin. People live underground in makeshift bunkers, and they struggle to provide food and protection for themselves. In the 1980s, this was a theme presented in other movies: *RoboCop* and *Blade Runner.* In these films, the future world has become a dark and littered place, instead of an advanced, clean, orderly environment. As technology advanced, critics wondered if this would truly lead to a better future, or a bleak existence.

The thesis statement for such a critique could be: *The Terminator* claims, as do other films of its time, that humanity's advancements would render a world of dark destruction rather than an improved, superior world.

Ellen Ripley, *right*, is a consultant for a group of marines who respond to an alien attack on planet LV-426.

5

An Overview of
Aliens

Aliens, the sequel to Ridley Scott's *Alien* (1979),
opens with Ellen Ripley being discovered in a
deep hypersleep aboard a drifting spacecraft. She
is the lone survivor of the *Nostromo*. The other crew
members met their grisly deaths in the previous film
on planet LV-426 at the hands of the aliens. Ripley
has been adrift in space for 57 years. She has not
aged, yet everyone else has.

Ripley has returned to Gateway Station, a space
station orbiting Earth, with no evidence of aliens or
the attack on LV-426. She is told that humans have
inhabited LV-426 for 20 years with no reports of
aliens. Ripley's flight license has been suspended
pending a psychiatric evaluation.

Soon, Carter Burke and Lieutenant Gorman of
the colonial marines, who wish to enlist her help,

approach Ripley. It seems those in charge of space settlements have lost contact with LV-426, home to some 60 to 75 families. Burke wants Ripley to accompany the team as a consultant when they travel to LV-426. Although Ripley initially refuses, she finally agrees to help Burke as long as he promises they are going back to destroy the aliens, not bring them back to study.

Returning to LV-426

Ripley, along with Burke, Gorman, and a group of battle-ready colonial marines, makes the journey back to LV-426 aboard the military transport ship *Sulaco*. The crew includes, among others: Sergeant Apone, the battle-hardened leader; Corporal Hicks, the capable, good-looking soldier; Private Vasquez, the muscular Latina who leads the pack with the M56 Smart Gun; Private Hudson, the mouthy troublemaker; and Bishop, an android. The team awakens from hypersleep chambers and prepares for their drop on LV-426. Heavily armed and confident, most of the marines seem to view the mission, and the thought of deadly aliens, as a joke.

The unit is deposited on LV-426, where they initially find no colonists. They do discover wreckage, however. In the medical bay, the unit discovers two living alien "facehuggers" in containment tanks. As Ripley had explained to the unit earlier, these parasites attach themselves to the face of a human host and deposit a type of embryo into the throat of the victim, where it incubates and eventually bursts through the chest of the victim as an alien "xenomorph," killing him or her.

The unit discovers a young girl, Rebecca Jordan, hiding. "Newt," as she says she is called, informs the group that all the others are dead. Lieutenant Gorman pries her for answers, but Newt opens up only after Ripley comforts the traumatized youngster. Newt says she wants to leave, but Ripley reassures the girl that she is safe with the group of soldiers. "It won't make any difference," the girl calmly warns.[1]

As Bishop dissects one of the parasites, Corporal Hicks picks up signals from the colonists' surgically implanted chips and discovers that the colonists are by the nuclear-power processing tower. Upon arrival, the team finds that the colonists have all been cocooned in some sort of secreted resin.

Ripley points out to Gorman that the marines must not fire their weapons. As they are directly under the primary heat exchangers, a bullet might rupture the cooling system and cause a thermal-nuclear explosion. The marines are instructed to use only flamethrowers.

The team finds a woman who is alive. Encased in the resin cocoon, she begs them to kill her, moments before an alien bursts through her chest. Apone uses the flamethrower on the alien, which ignites an alien attack on the unit. "Pull your team out, Gorman," Ripley warns, realizing the unit is about to be attacked by aliens.[2] As the fighting ensues, Gorman, Ripley, and Burke watch via the marines' helmet cameras back in the armored vehicle. Gorman freezes up, unable to give clear orders.

Finally, Ripley takes matters into her own hands and drives the armored vehicle toward the unit, crashing through a wall and rescuing the surviving Hicks, Hudson, and Vasquez. Gorman is knocked unconscious, and Hudson receives burns on his arm when he shoots an encroaching alien, splattering the alien's acid blood in the process.

Trapped

Ripley suggests that they leave and nuke the entire site. It is the only way to kill all the aliens.

The unit radios for the drop ship to return for them. However, a stowaway alien kills the pilots, and the vessel crashes. The survivors realize they are on their own and barricade themselves inside the complex. Ripley gets to work organizing a plan. Hicks is impressed with Ripley's abilities, and the two seem to bond. He gives Ripley his locator watch so that he can find her if they are separated.

After putting Newt to bed, Ripley discusses the alien parasite with Bishop. She insists that Bishop destroy the specimens, but Bishop informs her that Burke is adamant that the alien parasites be returned to the company's labs. A short while later, Bishop alerts the others that the processing station is greatly damaged and will self-detonate. Someone must make it outside to remote-pilot the remaining drop ship from the *Sulaco* to rescue them. Since Bishop is the nonhuman, he agrees to go.

Exhausted, Ripley joins Newt in the medical lab for some sleep. She awakens later to discover she and Newt are locked in, and the two alien facehuggers have been released. She successfully fights them off, and the two are rescued by the marines. Ripley then discovers Burke's wicked plot to smuggle the alien embryos past quarantine back on Earth inside herself and Newt. Before the team can decide what to do about Burke, they are attacked by aliens. All but Ripley, Hicks, and Newt are killed, and Newt is taken by an alien.

The Rescue

Ripley and Hicks rendezvous with Bishop, who lands the drop ship. Ripley gets the injured Hicks inside and tells Bishop they are not leaving without Newt. Ripley prepares for battle by taping together a pulse rifle and a flamethrower and grabbing handfuls of M40 grenades and marking flares. Bishop flies them to the processor and warns her they only have 19 minutes to evacuate before the nuclear reactor blows up.

A sweaty, determined Ripley enters the alien queen's nest. She had given Hicks' locator watch to Newt and uses it to track the girl. However, she finds the watch but no Newt. Upon hearing Newt scream, Ripley runs to her rescue and pulls her from a web of slimy resin. Carrying Newt, she runs to escape, only to find herself face-to-face with the alien queen. Standing precariously amid a field of alien eggs, Newt in one arm and her flamethrower in the other, Ripley carefully begins backing up and torches the eggs. The two then make a run for the drop ship amid explosions and fires throughout the processing center.

With the queen in pursuit, Ripley and Newt make it to the drop ship, and the four escape moments before the entire installation explodes in a nuclear blast. They make it to the *Sulaco,* only to find that the queen has hitched a ride on the ship's landing gear. The queen rips Bishop in half and then goes after the others. Ripley tells Newt to run and then secures herself behind an airlock door. She emerges wearing an exoskeletal cargo-loader. As the queen is ripping up the floor trying to get to Newt, Ripley throws out her famous battle cry, "Get away from her, you bitch!"[3] The two grapple, fighting and tumbling. They both fall into an airlock shaft. Ripley opens the door, sucking the queen into space, as she desperately hangs on to a ladder rung attached to the wall. She climbs up, and she and Newt embrace.

In the film's final scene, Ripley encloses Hicks and Bishop in hypersleep chambers and then tucks Newt into hers. The four sleeping survivors make their way back to Earth.

A poster for *Aliens* shows Ripley rescuing Newt.

6

How to Apply Feminist Criticism to *Aliens*

What Is Feminist Criticism?

Feminist criticism applies the ideas of feminism to a work. Feminism is the belief that women's opportunities and rights should equal those of men's. Historically, most cultures have been male dominated, or patriarchal. Feminist criticism strives to assess the work of art and to demonstrate whether common gender stereotypes exist within the work.

When critiquing a film from a feminist viewpoint, it is important to identify how the female characters are portrayed. Some might be portrayed in stereotypical roles of being the mother or caregiver, the beauty with little brains, or the intelligent bookworm who is socially awkward. Or, some movies might shake these longstanding female stereotypes. By applying feminist criticism, you can identify how these characters interact and how the society presented in the film perceives them.

Applying Feminist Criticism to *Aliens*

The female characters in Cameron's *Aliens* defy the typical gender norms. They are strong and courageous, adept at survival, and resourceful. Throughout the movie, Ellen Ripley, the main character, is portrayed as a strong woman, facing incomprehensible dangers and odds and is forced to step to the plate and successfully take charge where men have failed. She becomes caregiver to an orphaned girl, Newt. Although Ripley exudes love, compassion, and a territorial maternal instinct for the little girl, she does not lose a drop of her tough-as-nails fighting spirit. Cameron's *Aliens* depicts a society in which women can be strong, competent soldiers, career women, *and* still be loving caregivers and mothers.

Not only are the women perceived as equals to men in the film, they are often able to

Thesis Statement

The thesis statement is stated at the end of the first paragraph: "Cameron's *Aliens* depicts a society in which women can be strong, competent soldiers, career women, *and* still be loving caregivers and mothers."

overcome obstacles and handle
stressful situations better than
their male counterparts. When
the mission to return to LV-426
to search for missing colonists
commences, Ripley finds herself
working as a consultant among
a band of Colonial Marines. One
of only three female marines,
Private Vasquez is a confident,
well-muscled woman. Far from receiving special
treatment as a female, she is the wielder of the
smart gun and first to enter an unsecured room. She
is given full respect by her fellow male marines, one
of whom she is in a relationship with, and treated
(and teased) as one of the guys.

Ripley quickly emerges as a more apt leader
than the males. Throughout the movie, male Private
Hudson becomes frantic, emotional, and irrational
while dealing with the aliens. On more than one
occasion, Ripley needs to calm him down and
reassure him. When the group of marines becomes
ensnarled in their first desperate fight against the
vicious aliens, the casualties increase and chaos
ensues. Watching the mayhem on video monitors,

> **Argument One**
> The author begins to argue the thesis. Here is the first argument: "Not only are the women perceived as equals to men in the film, they are often able to overcome obstacles and handle stressful situations better than their male counterparts."

Lieutenant Gorman panics. Ripley tries to take control. "Pull your team out, Gorman!" she yells. "Do something!"[1] Seeing that he is too frightened to act, she steps in, rescuing the surviving soldiers. She is clearly a better leader than Gorman.

The men eventually respect Ripley's leadership ability. As the league of aliens close in on the survivors who are barricaded in the medical bay, Private Hicks, now in command, agrees to show Ripley how to use the M41-A pulse rifle, complete with grenade launcher. "Show me everything," Ripley tells Hicks. "I can handle myself."[2]

Argument Two

The author has turned to the second point of her thesis. She argues: "Along with her leadership skills, Ripley's maternal instincts become one of her most important skills."

Along with her leadership skills, Ripley's maternal instincts become one of her most important skills. Ripley's mothering ability is critical in the successful recovery of Newt in the first part of the film. When the team finds young Newt, she is scared and untrusting. Gorman tries to question the girl for answers, but he lacks the compassion and gentleness required to earn the girl's trust. Ripley coaxes the girl to come out of hiding and cares for her, feeding and cleaning her, and

Ripley's mothering ability helps her be successful.

reassures her that she's safe. Newt instantly bonds with Ripley, seeing her as a tender-yet-tough mother figure who will protect her. Handgun at the ready, Ripley tucks the little girl into bed, promises her she will not leave her, and agrees to sleep with her to help ward off her nightmares. Despite the group's precarious situation with the aliens on the loose, Ripley understands the child's needs.

In the final action scenes of the movie, only Newt, Hicks, Bishop, and Ripley remain. Running from encroaching aliens, Newt, Hicks, and Ripley race to make it to the transporter, where they will rendezvous with Bishop and evacuate the alien-infested LV-426. When Newt falls to the level below and is taken by an alien, Ripley is tested. Should she write her off as gone, as they were forced to do with the others, or risk the safety of the survivors to rescue her? Ripley's mother-like connection to Newt accelerates her bravery, making her the only one confident enough to try to save the young girl. Bishop warns Ripley they have only 19 minutes to evacuate before the nuclear reactor blows up. Ripley replies, "She's alive. There's still time."[3] Ripley is the only one willing to risk her life and the lives of the remaining few to go back to rescue Newt. She loads

> **Argument Three**
> Next, the author explains how Ripley's motherly instincts help her be strong. She argues: "Ripley's mother-like connection to Newt accelerates her bravery, making her the only one confident enough to try to save the young girl."

up on the transporter's largest, deadliest weapons and walks straight into the alien queen's nest to rescue Newt.

<u>Ripley does not need to relinquish her role as a mother to be a powerful warrior.</u> Upon finding Newt, she frees the girl from the cocoon in which she is trapped. In one of the movie's most iconic scenes, we see Ripley, flamethrower on one arm and carrying Newt with the other. She is both warrior and mother. Standing in the middle of countless alien eggs, Ripley faces off with the queen, pointing her flamethrower at the eggs.

> **Argument Four**
>
> Here, the author focuses on how the two traits, "mother" and "warrior," of Ripley's personality come together, allowing her to rescue Newt.

The final fight scene in *Aliens* reinforces the concept of power and motherhood coexisting. Upon discovering the queen attached to the transporter once they disembark the ship, the battle begins anew. Donning the robotic power-loader suit, Ripley prepares for battle. Defeating the alien queen and dispensing her into deep space, a bleeding and battered Ripley retrieves Newt. Exhausted, Ripley has emerged as the only member of the crew able to kill the vicious, snarling alien and save everyone on the ship.

Conclusion

The final paragraph concludes the author's critique and sums up the arguments that support the assertion of the thesis.

Throughout Cameron's *Aliens,* we see a society where women are strong, capable, and equal in their abilities to the men, yet they still retain traditional feminine roles of mothers and caregivers. The men have no qualms about allowing a woman to lead them into battle, establish a fight plan, and dispense orders. The duty of ensuring their survival is left to the most capable, regardless of gender. When forced to choose between the evacuation of the survivors and the rescue of her surrogate daughter, Ripley is adamant that there is time for both, proving that she will budge neither on her mothering instinct nor on her power and leadership. Ripley proves that motherhood does not necessitate a woman sacrificing her professional authority.

Thinking Critically about *Aliens*

Now it is your turn to assess the critique. Consider these questions:

1. The author claims that *Aliens* shows women can be both powerful and motherly. Do you agree with this interpretation of the film? Why or why not?

2. Part of the author's argument asserts that the women in the film are just as capable, if not more capable, of survival as their male counterparts. Do you agree? Why or why not?

3. Does the film prove anything else about women or men? Is there an important piece of evidence or counterevidence that the author ignores?

Other Approaches

The critique you have just read is merely one way to approach *Aliens* through the lens of feminist criticism. What are some other ways to apply this approach to the film? Following are two different ways to apply feminist criticism to *Aliens*.

Women Are the Only Caregivers

Aliens may reinforce the concept that women stereotypically fill the role of mothers and caregivers in the private world, while men focus primarily on tasks in the public world such as taking on careers. For example, Ripley is the one who coaxes Newt out of hiding, cares for her, and saves her life. The male soldiers take very little notice of Newt and have almost no interaction with her.

Such a critique might have the thesis statement: *Aliens* reinforces the stereotype that women are the natural caregivers and mothers, while men have little interest in caring for children.

A Woman's Function Is Procreator

The climax of *Aliens* involves Ripley battling the queen alien, who is protecting her eggs. It could be argued from a feminist standpoint that the movie reinforces the stereotype that women serve to give birth to the future generations of a species, be that human or otherwise. The queen's main concern is protecting her eggs, and upon Ripley's destruction of those eggs, revenge.

The thesis statement for such a critique could be: *Aliens* reinforces the idea that women's greatest strengths are realized only if they embrace their maternal instincts.

Titanic debuted in theaters in 1997.

7

An Overview of
Titanic

Titanic opens with a team of deep-sea explorers, led
by Brock Lovett, sending submersibles down to the
ocean floor where the remains of the *Titanic* rest.
Lovett hopes to maneuver through the wreckage
to find the safe of Cal Hockley, which he believes
still holds the *Coeur de la Mer,* or "Heart of the
Ocean," a 56-carat blue diamond necklace. Instead
of finding the necklace, Lovett discovers a drawing
of a nude woman wearing it.

Rose Dawson Calvert, an elderly woman, sees
Lovett's discovery on the news and phones him to
say that she is the woman in the picture. Intrigued,
Lovett flies Rose and her granddaughter Lizzy to
the salvage ship to hear her story of the night of
April 14, 1912, the night both the sketch was drawn
and the *Titanic* sank. Although there is no record

of a Rose Dawson as a passenger, Rose begins to recount her story.

Back to *Titanic*

The scene fades from present-day 1996 to April 10, 1912, the day the *Titanic* set sail from Southampton, England. A 17-year-old Rose DeWitt Bukater boards the *Titanic*, along with her wealthy fiancé, Cal Hockley, and her mother, Ruth. Meanwhile, Jack Dawson and his friend Fabrizio win third-class tickets for the *Titanic* in a poker game.

As the voyage gets under way, it is clear that Cal is attempting to control Rose. But as Rose's father has died and left her mother and her very indebted, Ruth is adamant that Rose marry Cal in order to remedy their financial straits. Rose is desperate to flee the forced marriage. After dinner on the ship, she runs to the stern of the ship, crying, and prepares to jump off. Jack sees the young lady and attempts to talk her back off the railing. He ends up saving her life when she slips.

The following day, the two spend time together. Jack shows her his drawings and tells her of his life as a drifter. That evening, Jack joins Rose, Cal,

Ruth, and some other first-class passengers for
dinner. Afterward, he and Rose meet. Jack takes
Rose below deck, where the third-class passengers
are dancing and drinking. Cal has sent his valet,
Mr. Lovejoy, to follow Rose. He discovers her
having a good time with Jack. The following
morning, Cal becomes violent with Rose. Realizing
she cannot spend her life with him, Rose meets
Jack on the bow of the ship. The two return to
her stateroom, where Rose pays Jack to sketch
her wearing nothing but the Heart of the Ocean
diamond pendant that Cal presented to her as an
engagement gift.

Rose places the drawing in Cal's safe, and the
two escape the room just as Lovejoy comes looking
for them. He chases the young couple, who run
through the boiler room to evade him. They hide in
the storage room, where they make love in a car.

The Sinking

The couple then runs to the forward-well deck,
where Rose tells Jack that when the ship docks
in New York, she plans to get off with him. They
are present when the *Titanic* hits the iceberg and
overhear an officer telling the captain that the

forward hull is buckled, and the ship is taking on
water. Rose decides they should tell her mother
and Cal, but when they arrive at the suite of rooms,
Lovejoy slips the diamond necklace into Jack's
pocket, enabling Cal, who is furious upon finding
the nude sketch of his fiancée, to accuse Jack of
stealing it.

Jack is apprehended by the master-at-arms and
locked up. Meanwhile, Rose and Ruth prepare
to board a lifeboat, as it has been ascertained by
Thomas Andrews, the ship's architect, that the ship
will sink within one to two hours. However, Rose
refuses to join her mother on the lifeboat, as it
would mean leaving Jack behind.

Rose battles her way to the E Deck, where she
finds Jack handcuffed to a pipe. Unable to find
the key to the handcuffs, she frees him by use of
a fire axe, and the two race to make it back to the
lifeboats. The stairway gates have been locked,
however, imprisoning the third-class passengers.
Jack enlists the help of Fabrizio and Tommy Ryan,
another friend, to break through the gates.

Jack and Rose find a lifeboat, and Jack urges
Rose to get on it. She refuses to go without him.
Cal joins them, reassuring Rose that there is another

boat on the opposite side that both he and Jack can board, per a financial arrangement he has made with an officer. Cal puts his coat on Rose, and she is lowered in the lifeboat. Cal then tells Jack he will not benefit from the lifeboat arrangement.

As the *Titanic* sinks, Jack and Rose struggle to survive.

However, Rose jumps off her lifeboat, and she and Jack reunite on the deck below. Seeing the two lovers hugging and kissing, Cal becomes mad with jealousy and pulls a gun chasing after them. Rose and Jack flee down several flights of stairs and become trapped below. As the waters quickly rise, the two break free and make their way back up to the ship's top deck.

As chaos ensues with people desperate to board lifeboats, Cal grabs a small abandoned girl and takes a seat on the last lifeboat with her. With the entire bow of the boat underwater, the ship begins to fully flood until the front half of the ship breaks away and sinks. All around them, Rose and Jack see people falling to their deaths or drowning. Along with a mass of other passengers, they rush to the stern, desperate to hang on. The stern goes down, pulling Jack and Rose under. They swim their way back to the surface, and Jack helps Rose on top of a floating wooden panel. He tries to climb up, but it will only support the weight of one person. Jack hangs on to the panel, and the two await the return of the lifeboats.

Rose tells Jack that she loves him, and he answers by insisting that she not say her good-byes, that she will not die this night, but rather as an old lady, warm in her bed. He goes on to profess his love to her.

By the time the lifeboat finally returns looking for survivors, Rose discovers Jack has died of hypothermia. She is rescued and taken aboard the

RMS *Carpathia*, where she gives her name as Rose
Dawson. Cal is also aboard the *Carpathia*. As he
searches for her, Rose manages to keep her face
hidden from his sight.

The Heart of the Ocean

That night, after she finishes telling Lovett,
his team, and her granddaughter Lizzy about her
experience aboard the *Titanic*, Rose walks out to
the stern of the ship. In her hand, she holds the
Heart of the Ocean diamond necklace, which she
had discovered in the pocket of Cal's coat she was
wearing when rescued. A smile on her face, Rose
drops the necklace into the ocean. The scene cuts
to Rose, asleep in her bed. Surrounding her are
pictures of her life, a life filled with adventure
and experiences she and Jack had talked about. In
what can be either interpreted as a dream or Rose's
death, a young Rose meets Jack at the clock on
the Grand Staircase of the *Titanic*, surrounded by
the passengers who perished. The two kiss as the
assembly claps.

Jack and Rose come from different social classes.

How to Apply Marxist Criticism to *Titanic*

What Is Marxist Criticism?

Marxist criticism is a theory that traces its roots back to the influential writings of Karl Marx and Friedrich Engels, both nineteenth-century Germans whose ideas and writings helped shape modern communism and socialism. Marx and Engels' theories suggest that throughout the course of human history, the working class has struggled to attain equality and fairness, yet falls short. Marxist theory also states that literature, religion, and the other cultural frameworks are shaped by economic and social conditions instead of the other way around.

Marxist critics look at class struggle and economics as reflected in the work. A book, film, piece of music, or art is interpreted in relation to relevance regarding the depiction of class struggle within the work. Additionally, the Marxist critic also asks the question: does the work agree with social norms of the time, or does it subvert them?

Applying Marxist Criticism to *Titanic*

Cameron's epic love story *Titanic* tells the tale of two teenagers from very divergent class backgrounds who board and meet on the ill-fated RMS *Titanic*. Rose DeWitt Bukater, an upper-class young lady, is bound for the United States along with her snobbish mother and wealthy fiancé, Cal Hockley. Jack Dawson, an orphaned, poor drifter, is also bound for the United States. The two meet and fall in love, but those around them are at the ready to point out the vast chasm between first class and steerage. Cameron's story of the two lovers goes beyond the struggle they will face when the ship hits an iceberg, and they are forced to face the freezing waters of the Atlantic Ocean. *Titanic* asserts that the class hierarchy is arbitrary since a person's actions or character should be the measure of his or her worth.

Thesis Statement

The thesis statement is stated at the end of the first paragraph: "*Titanic* asserts that the class hierarchy is arbitrary since a person's actions or character should be the measure of his or her worth."

Returning to the United States to wed the wealthy Cal, Rose and her company's travel arrangements reflect their upper-class status. She and the other first-class passengers are allowed to skip the health inspections demanded of the lower-class passengers and may board the ship upon arrival. They are immediately whisked to their suites of luxury, where maids place vases of freshly cut flowers and crewmen deliver their luggage. But despite all the trappings of extravagant wealth, her station in life has been secretly diminished by her father's financial mistakes. Through her engagement to Cal, Rose maintains an upper-class lifestyle.

Similarly, Jack's accommodations on the ship reveal his lower-class status and make it clear that the society views him as "unfit" for Rose. Jack and his friend Fabrizio board the ship and make their way to steerage, where multiple

Argument One

The author begins to argue the thesis with this statement: "Returning to the United States to wed the wealthy Cal, Rose and her company's travel arrangements reflect their upper-class status."

Argument Two

Now the author has turned to discussing the class status of the other main character—Jack. She asserts: "Similarly, Jack's accommodations on the ship reveal his lower-class status and make it clear that the society views him as 'unfit' for Rose."

bunks per room await them. There, they meet other working-class passengers who are seeking a better life in America—lives that unquestionably will involve hard work, fortitude, and no entitlements. As Jack and Fabrizio relax on deck, they meet an Irish lad named Tommy Ryan. The three commiserate about the first-class passengers' dogs being brought down to the second-class promenade deck to relieve themselves. Jack brushes it off, joking, "Ah, it lets us know where we rank in the scheme of things." "Like we could forget?" Tommy retorts, laughing.[1] The young men see Rose for the first time up on the first-class promenade deck above, and Jack is immediately smitten. "Oh, forget it, boyo," Tommy advises him. "You'd as like have angels fly out your arse as get next to the likes of her."[2]

Meanwhile, Rose's engagement to Cal reveals that sustaining one's class status can be dangerous and unhealthy. Rose is expected to marry Cal for his wealth, and to maintain her and her mother's social position. Rose's mother, Ruth,

> **Argument Three**
> Here, the author exposes the dangers of the class hierarchy. She explains: "Meanwhile, Rose's engagement to Cal reveals that sustaining one's class status can be dangerous and unhealthy."

reiterates to Rose that the only choice they have is a marriage between her and Cal. "It will ensure our survival," Ruth urges.[3] Ruth is not concerned with her daughter's unhappiness at the thought of marrying a temperamental, overbearing man. Her interests lie with keeping up appearances and reestablishing their wealth. When Rose asks her mother why the burden is put upon her to marry Cal, her mother responds, asking, "Do you want to see me working as a seamstress? To see all our fine things sold at auction?"[4] Ruth knows that if Rose does not marry into wealth, she and her daughter

Even though Cal, *right*, is part of the higher class, he is not an admirable person.

will find themselves among the poor working class. For Ruth, that is a horrific thought. However, it is clear that Rose's marriage to Cal would not be a happy or healthy one for her. Cal physically and emotionally abuses Rose. He slaps her across the face and grabs her roughly several times throughout the film. Although Cal matches Rose's class status, it is clear that he is not a good person.

> **Argument Four**
> The author addresses the point that: "Jack is more admirable than Cal, although many distrust him due to his lower-class status."

As Rose and Jack get to know each other, it becomes clear that Jack is more admirable than Cal, although many distrust him due to his lower-class status. Unlike Cal, Jack is interested in learning about Rose as a person. However, most of the characters in the upper class distrust Jack. Even after Jack talks Rose down from the railing and rescues her from falling into the water, he is suspected of some nefarious deed. As the master-at-arms shackles Jack, Cal demands to know why Jack thought he could lay his hands on Rose. Rose must step in to explain that Jack saved her life.

Jack is not the only one judged for his class background. Molly Brown, a wealthy first-class passenger, was not born into the upper class, so she is not accepted by the aristocracy as one of their own despite her admirable qualities. Rose explains of Molly, "Her husband had struck gold some place out West, and she was what mother called 'New Money.'"[5] When Jack is invited to supper with the first-class passengers as reward for saving Rose, Rose's mother and Cal go out of their way to try to embarrass Jack. They clearly see him as inferior and beneath them. The only person of the dining group who is genuinely kind to Jack is Molly. She even gives Jack nice clothing to wear to the dinner. However, the upper-class women dislike Molly. The Countess of Rothes calls Molly "that vulgar Brown woman."[6] Even though Molly, like Jack, seems to be a good person, she is judged by her former social standing.

> **Argument Five**
>
> The author further supports her last argument by adding to it. She asserts: "Molly Brown, a wealthy first-class passenger, was not born into the upper class, so she is not accepted by the aristocracy as one of their own despite her admirable qualities."

After the sinking of the ship at the end of the film, Rose and Jack cling to hope as they await the return of the lifeboats in the freezing waters. However, by the time the only boat returns, Jack has succumbed

Argument Six

The author uses a final argument to demonstrate that Rose's only escape from class expectations is to turn her back on the upper class and lower her societal standing for the sake of freedom.

Conclusion

The final paragraph concludes the author's critique and sums up the arguments that support the assertion of the thesis.

to hypothermia. Aboard the RMS *Carpathia*, Rose has the chance to reunite with Cal, who has also survived. However, realizing that class status is not the measure of a person's worth, Rose chooses to forfeit a "privileged" life of aristocracy and to pursue her true desires. She takes Jack's last name. No longer encumbered by the expectations placed upon her, she lives out her days as an actress and pursues a myriad of other adventurous experiences Jack had spoken of aboard the *Titanic*.

Throughout the film, both Jack and Rose encounter many instances of class divisions. Members of their own classes place assumptions as well as expectations upon them, and Jack learns the hard lesson that even by rescuing a privileged first-class lady, he is still rewarded with cool contempt from members of her class. In the end, *Titanic* makes it clear that a person's class status does not determine their true worth.

Thinking Critically about *Titanic*

Now it is your turn to assess the critique. Consider these questions:

1. The thesis claims that *Titanic* points out the arbitrary nature of the class hierarchy. Do you agree with this thesis? Why or why not?

2. At the end of the critique, the author argues that Rose decides to leave her high-class status because she realizes that class status is not a measure of a person's worth. Do you agree?

3. *Titanic* takes places in the early twentieth century. Do you think class status is as important to people today? Why or why not?

Other Approaches

The critique you have just read is merely one way to approach *Titanic* through the lens of a Marxist critique. What are some other ways to apply this approach? Recall that Marxist criticism views the work within the context of societal class and economics. Here are two alternate approaches.

Happiness Is Independence

One could argue that Jack Dawson's penniless, happy, full-of-life existence mirrors Marx's belief that, "A being only considers himself independent when he stands on his own feet; and he only stands on his own feet when he owes his existence to himself."[7] Repeatedly during the film, Jack points out that he has no money and that he does not know where his life is headed, but he is grateful that he has what he needs and that he believes life to be a gift to be embraced.

Such a critique might have the thesis statement: Jack's bohemian existence reaffirms the Marxist tenet that happiness is not the result of wealth or private property, but rather true independence from both.

The Futility of Material Wealth

Titanic may also make a point about the futility of material wealth. There are several examples of this within the film. Cal attempts to buy Rose's love with a 56-carat diamond necklace and promises of anything she desires. She, however, chooses a poor third-class passenger over him. Additionally, as the ship sinks, wealthy men such as John J. Astor and Benjamin Guggenheim, along with the very poor, lose their lives. In the film's final scene, Rose drops the Heart of the Ocean into the Atlantic, symbolizing that the necklace, worth a fortune, held only the sentimental value Rose gave it the night Jack drew her wearing nothing but the necklace.

The thesis statement for such a critique could be: *Titanic* exemplifies the idea that material wealth cannot decide a person's future, and it is not as important as human connections and emotion.

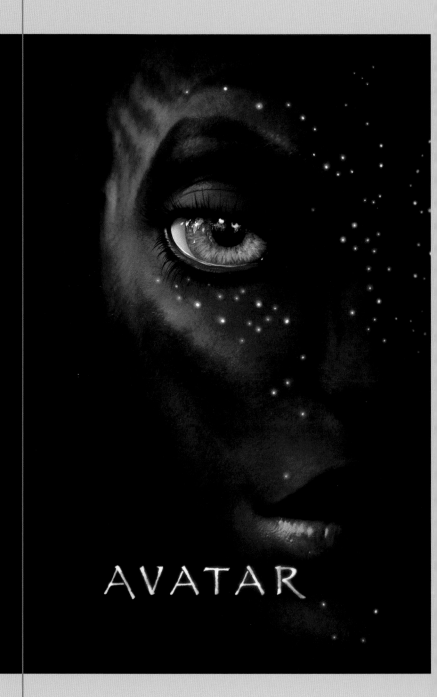

Avatar opened in 2009.

9

An Overview of
Avatar

Avatar opens as Jake Sully, a paraplegic and former
marine, emerges from nearly six years in cryosleep
aboard a ship bound for the moon Pandora, located
in the Alpha Centauri star system. The year is 2154
AD. Through a voiceover, he explains that his twin
brother, Tom, a gifted scientist, was mugged and
murdered. The RDA Corporation, Tom's employer,
offers Jake his brother's position as an avatar
operator.

The Avatar Program, a division of the RDA
Corporation and headed by the outspoken Dr. Grace
Augustine, is tasked with assisting with diplomacy
between the native Na'vi and the "Sky People,"
as the Na'vi call the humans. They do so by
utilizing avatar bodies they grow from fusing a
combination of Na'vi and human DNA. Each avatar

is genetically matched to the human who will be operating it through a mental link inside a chamber. Since they were identical twins, their genomes being identical, Jake will be able to operate his brother's avatar. Arriving at the laboratory along with Jake is scientist Norm Spellman. Grace is displeased with Jake's presence, arguing that he knows nothing about science. Yet, Jake immediately takes to his avatar form.

The Na'vi

As Grace, Norm, and Jake collect samples in the rainforest in their avatar forms, they are separated when Jake is attacked and pursued by a thanator, Pandora's apex land predator. He escapes but is lost in the rainforest and must survive the night until the search can be continued the next morning.

Nighttime falls, and as a pack of black-skinned viperwolves descends upon Jake, a female Na'vi warrior named Neytiri comes to his rescue. Disgusted with Jake's incompetence in the forest, she initially refuses to help him any further. However, as delicate seeds of the Sacred Tree descend upon Jake, Neytiri decides to take Jake to Hometree, a mammoth tree that serves as the dwelling of the Omaticaya, her people. There, Neytiri presents Jake to her father, Eytukan, the clan chief, and her mother, Mo'at, spiritual leader of the clan who interprets the will of Eywa, the mother goddess worshipped by the Na'vi. Mo'at assigns her daughter the job of showing "Jakesully" the ways of the Na'vi.

As Jake's avatar falls asleep in a large leaf hammock, his human body awakens. Grace is surprised to learn that the Omaticaya have chosen Jake. Norm is obviously jealous. However, Jake had previously met with RDA's head of security, Colonel Miles Quaritch. Quaritch asked Jake to

Neytiri, *right*, teaches Jake, *left in his avatar form*, the ways of the Na'vi.

provide him with information about the Na'vi. He promises Jake, "You get me what I need, I'll see to it you get your legs back when you rotate home. Your real legs."[1] He later tells Jake that the Omaticaya village is resting on the richest unobtainium deposit around. It is Quaritch's job to get the Na'vi to move so that the mineral can be mined freely.

Discovering that Jake is talking with Quaritch, Grace moves herself, Norm, and Jake to a remote outpost located high in the floating mountains. The team spends three months there, while Jake links up to his avatar and is taught the ways of the Na'vi by Neytiri. Neytiri also teaches him the Na'vi's beliefs and harmonious existence with nature. She then deems him ready to perform the Na'vi rite of passage, the taming of the flying banshee, at which he succeeds. Afterward, Jake is initiated into the tribe. That night, he and Neytiri choose each other as mates.

An Attack

The following morning, RDA bulldozers appear and knock down the Tree of Voices that is sacred to the Na'vi. Jake breaks the cameras off the equipment, enraging Quaritch. Grace tries to reason with RDA administrator Parker Selfridge. However, Quaritch uses one of Jake's video log entries, in which Jake states the Na'vi will never leave Hometree, to convince Selfridge to use force. Quaritch and Selfridge plan to destroy Hometree.

Pilot Trudy Chacon informs Grace that Quaritch is rolling the gunships to Hometree. Grace finally resorts to asking Selfridge if he wants to be responsible for killing Na'vi children. Selfridge allows Grace and Jake to link up to their avatars to give the Na'vi one hour's warning to evacuate.

In their avatar forms, Grace and Jake plead with the Na'vi people to leave Hometree to avoid a certain death, and Jake finally admits to Neytiri that he was sent to learn their ways. Betrayed, Neytiri yells at Jake, "You will never be one of the people!"[2] Grace's and Jake's avatars are then tied up as Quaritch's gunships move toward Hometree.

As Quaritch's fleet of war ships unleash gas canisters and then incendiary rounds to flush them out, the Na'vi stand their ground with bows and arrows, which merely clatter off the ships. Finally, Hometree is bombed and falls to the ground, burning. Many Na'vi die as a result of the attack, including Neytiri's father, Eytukan. The Na'vi retreat through the forest to the Tree of Souls.

Meanwhile, back at the RDA facility, Selfridge orders Jake and Grace to be unplugged from their avatars and placed in lockup along with Norm. Trudy frees them, and the foursome escape in Trudy's Scorpion aircraft. However, Quaritch unloads his sidearm at the escaping group, and Grace is shot in the abdomen. Trudy flies them to the remote linkup post, where Jake relinks with his avatar. He realizes he has one chance to win back the trust of the Na'vi. Flying his banshee, he jumps on the back of and tames the toruk, the mighty flying predator. Only five times in history has a Na'vi warrior bonded with the "Last Shadow." Jake and the toruk land among the Na'vi gathered around the Tree of Souls. Jake asks Mo'at to help Grace. The clan performs a ritual, asking Eywa to permanently transfer Grace from her dying human body into her avatar. But it is too late. Grace dies.

Jake rallies the Na'vi, asking them to fly out to all of the tribes, telling them *Toruk Macto*, the "Rider of Last Shadow," calls for them to come.[3] All the Na'vi join forces to fight the Quaritch and his forces who plan to attack the Tree of Souls, believing its destruction will completely demoralize the natives. Jake prays to Eywa, asking for her help with the upcoming battle. The following morning, Quaritch's gunships mobilize and enter the Flux Vortex, where the Tree of Souls—and the Na'vi troops—await. Riding the toruk, Jake's avatar leads the banshee-riding warriors, while Norm's avatar rides with the direhorse warriors. Trudy is killed, along with countless Na'vi. As Neytiri looks on at her fallen comrades, the animals of Pandora join the fray as reinforcements, overcoming the RDA troops.

Quaritch escapes his exploding ship in a robotic exoskeletal AMP suit. He and Jake's avatar engage in a fight. Quaritch smashes the linkup unit where Jake's human body resides, exposing him to the planet's poisonous atmospheric gases. Just as Quaritch moves to kill Jake's avatar, Neytiri shoots two arrows through him, killing him. She finds Jake's human body in time to place an air mask over his face, saving his life.

In the end, most of the humans leave Pandora, but some, including Jake and Norm, stay there. In the final scene, Mo'at performs the ritual at the Tree of Spirits that transfers Jake permanently into his avatar body.

When Jake links up to his avatar and joins the Na'vi people, he realizes the value of their culture.

How to Apply Postcolonial Criticism to *Avatar*

What Is Postcolonial Criticism?

Postcolonial criticism is a style analysis that gained popularity in the 1960s. According to critical theory scholar Charles Bressler, postcolonial criticism "can be defined as an approach to literary analysis that concerns itself particularly with literature written in English in formerly colonized countries."[1] These colonized locations include Australia, New Zealand, Africa, and South America. Postcolonial criticism may also be applied to film.

One of the primary focuses of postcolonial analysis is examining what happens when one culture takes over another culture. Particularly, postcolonial criticism addresses the results of the introduction of Western ideology on indigenous peoples.

Applying Postcolonial Criticism to *Avatar*

Avatar is a futuristic story of a marine who joins a mission to a distant moon where humans mining a precious and very rare metal are in conflict with the indigenous people. The protagonist soon finds himself torn between fulfilling his military orders and protecting a way of life he grows to accept and love. With its focus on Jake Sully's infiltration of the Na'vi tribe, along with its villainous representation of materialism and capitalism at the expense of the indigenous people, *Avatar* depicts the dangers of colonization as well as the benefits of learning about a civilization rather than colonizing it.

From the beginning of the movie, it is clear that the Avatar Program largely benefits the colonizers—*not* the colonized. When Jake arrives on Pandora to participate in the program, the colony's administrator, Parker Selfridge, says

Thesis Statement

The author's thesis statement appears at the end of the first paragraph: "With its focus on Jake Sully's infiltration of the Na'vi tribe, along with its villainous representation of materialism and capitalism at the expense of the indigenous people, *Avatar* depicts the dangers of colonization as well as the benefits of learning about a civilization rather than colonizing it."

Argument One

The author illustrates the problems with Grace and Selfridge's intentions with the Na'vi.

to Grace Augustine, the program's leader, "You're supposed to be winning the hearts and minds of the natives. . . . You look like them, and you talk like them and they'll start trusting us."[2] Selfridge makes it clear that the true purpose behind creating the avatars is to help keep the peace with the locals so that mining of the precious metal can continue on Pandora. By setting up schools and teaching the Na'vi English, it may at first appear that Grace and Selfridge are helping the Na'vi. But Grace is teaching the native children human-based knowledge, or rather, what is viewed as important to humans, not to the Na'vi. The humans think that the Na'vi need education. However, many of the humans in charge fail to recognize that the Na'vi have their own culture and intelligence and do not need a human education for their livelihood.

Meanwhile, it is clear that Selfridge and Colonel Miles Quaritch are content with killing the Na'vi and wiping out their homes if need be for financial gain and greed. As the movie progresses, Selfridge tells Jake, "Look, killing

> **Argument Two**
> Here, the author reinforces the argument that Selfridge and Quaritch are driven by "financial gain and greed," regardless of the ramifications to the natives.

the indigenous looks bad, but there's one thing that shareholders hate more than bad press, and that's a bad quarterly statement."[3] As Selfridge and Quaritch continue their campaign to rid the area of the indigenous people, they lose any respect for nature and life. While the Na'vi live off the land, taking only what they need and killing only when necessary, Quaritch's troops come in with bulldozers, prepared to strip the land in an effort to access the mineral they seek to mine.

Argument Three

The author uses the next argument to depict the final result of the "human's greed, disregard for nature, and the belief in their own species' superiority."

In the end, the human's greed, disregard for nature, and the belief in their own species' superiority ultimately lead to the tragic downfall of both the Na'vi and the human military. The military sets its sights on destroying the Na'vi's settlement, Hometree, and then their sacred Tree of Souls in an attempt to drive off the Na'vi. But the military underestimates the resolve of the Na'vi to fight following the incineration of Hometree, resulting in a brutal battle with countless casualties on both sides. By the end of the film, the Na'vi have lost their home, a large portion of their lands, and many tribe members, including Eytukan. The humans also have many casualties.

The character of Jake shows the importance of understanding a culture on its own terms. Jake's experience makes the claim that learning about a new culture, rather than imposing the views of one's own culture upon it, can lead to understanding, success, and friendship. Upon entering the Na'vi tribe's settlement, Jake is brought before the elders. Although Jake comes from a technologically superior culture, he is defenseless in the forest and needs Neytiri's help to survive. Neytiri's mother gives her the task of teaching Jake the ways of the Na'vi people. This includes hunting, riding, language, beliefs, and all other aspects of the Na'vi culture. Jake not only learns these things, but masters many of them. He becomes the sixth Na'vi warrior in history to bond with the mighty predator toruk, earning him a spot of great honor among the Na'vi. Because Jake is willing to embrace the Na'vi culture, rather than impose his own culture upon it, he is successful at Na'vi rituals and tasks.

> **Argument Four**
>
> The author further supports her thesis by pointing out an example of what happens when a character attempts to understand a culture, rather than impose his or her own views upon it.

Neytiri helps
Jake realize the
Na'vi's value.

Furthermore, his open-mindedness to learning about the Na'vi tribe brings him closer to Neytiri.

Avatar demonstrates how the effects of colonization on a culture, and the application of the Western world's ways of thinking, can lead to the destruction of that culture. But *Avatar* also teaches the audience how cultures might be able to peacefully collide, using the character of Jake as a model. Jake's experience with the Na'vi is an example of how cultures can learn from each other when they are open-minded.

Conclusion
The final paragraph concludes the author's critique and sums up the arguments that support the assertion of the thesis.

Thinking Critically about *Avatar*

Now it is your turn to assess the critique. Consider these questions:

1. The author claims that *Avatar* depicts the dangers of colonization and how those dangers lead to the destruction of a culture. Do you agree with this thesis? Why or not why?

2. As part of her supporting argument, the author claims that Jake is able to excel at the Na'vi's way of life because he is open to learning about the culture. Do you agree? Why or why not?

3. What was the most interesting argument made? What was the weakest? Is there anything you could add to the critique to make it a stronger argument?

Other Approaches

The critique you have just read is merely one way to apply postcolonial criticism to the film *Avatar*. What are some other ways to apply this approach? Remember that postcolonial criticism focuses on the effects of colonization on a society. Here are two alternate approaches.

Reinforcing Colonial Fantasy

In contrast to the reality of the postcolonization of most cultures, Cameron's story concludes with the Na'vi ridding their world of the colony of humans who have come to exploit Pandora for material gain. They do this, however, under the leadership of a white male who was once their enemy. The depiction of a white male "savior" is one that is seen in other works of literature and films, such as *Dances with Wolves*, *Pocahontas*, and *The Last Samurai*.

The thesis statement for such a critique could be: *Avatar* reinforces the colonialist fantasy that the salvation of a colonized group of indigenous people can only come at the hands of a Westerner who has a change of heart and leads the people to victory.

Science versus Nature

Some critics point out that a common theme in postcolonialist works is the view that colonized indigenous tribes are simplistic "nature people," whereas the colonizers have scientific superiority, consisting of medicine, tools, and technology. In this line of thinking, colonizers believe they are justified to subdue the natives in the name of progress, yet they underestimate the knowledge and benefits of the nature of the relationship with the indigenous people.

A possible thesis statement for such a critique could be: *Avatar* demonstrates the skewed colonial ideology that conquering a seemingly uncivilized people in the name of progress is noble, yet in reality, strips the colonized people of some of their greatest attributes.

You Critique It

Now that you have learned about several different critical theories and how to apply them to film, are you ready to perform a critique of your own? You have read that this type of evaluation can help you look at movies from a new perspective and make you pay attention to issues you may not have otherwise recognized. So, why not use one of the critical theories profiled in this book to consider a fresh take on your favorite movie?

First, choose a theory and the movie you want to analyze. Remember that the theory is a springboard for asking questions about the work.

Next, write a specific question that relates to the theory you have selected. Then you can form your thesis, which should provide the answer to that question. Your thesis is the most important part of your critique and offers an argument about the work based on the tenets, or beliefs, of the theory you are applying. Recall that the thesis statement typically appears at the very end of the introductory paragraph of your essay. It is usually only one sentence long.

After you have written your thesis, find evidence to back it up. Good places to start are in the work itself or journals or articles that discuss what other people have said about it. Since you are critiquing a movie, you may also want to read about the director's life to get a sense of what factors may have affected the creative process. This can be useful if working within historical or auteur types of criticism.

Depending on which theory you apply you can often find evidence in the movie's language, plot, or character development. You should also explore parts of the movie that seem to disprove your thesis and create an argument against them. As you do this, you might want to address what other critics have written about the movie. Their quotes may help support your claim.

Before you start analyzing a work, think about the different arguments made in this book. Reflect on how evidence supporting the thesis was presented. Did you find that some of the techniques used to back up the arguments were more convincing than others? Try these methods as you prove your thesis in your own critique.

When you are finished writing your critique, read it over carefully. Is your thesis statement understandable? Do the supporting arguments flow logically, with the topic of each paragraph clearly stated? Can you add any information that would present your readers with a stronger argument in favor of your thesis? Were you able to use quotes from the movie, as well as from other critics, to enhance your ideas?

Did you see the work in a new light?

Timeline

1954 James Cameron is born in Kapuskasing, Ontario, Canada, on August 16.

1984 *The Terminator,* written and directed by Cameron, is released and becomes a hit, opening at the number one spot at the box office.

1986 Cameron's science-fiction action hit *Aliens* hits the big screen and wins Academy Awards for best visual effects and best sound effects.

1989 Cameron takes viewers on an underwater special-effects adventure with the release of *The Abyss,* which earns him four Oscar nominations.

1991 Cameron furthers his success with the release of *Terminator 2: Judgment Day.*

1993 Cameron's fourth wife, Linda Hamilton, gives birth to a daughter, Josephine Archer Cameron, on February 15.

1997 Cameron's film *Titanic* is released on December 19. It breaks box office records, taking home 11 Oscars.

1968 Cameron's interest in special effects is sparked when he sees Stanley Kubrick's film *2001: A Space Odyssey.*

1971 Cameron moves with his family to California, and enrolls at Fullerton College.

1977 Cameron cocreates his first film, the 12-minute *Xenogenesis.*

1978 Cameron marries his first wife, Sharon Williams, on February 14.

1979 Roger Corman's New World Pictures studio hires Cameron as a miniature model builder.

1980 Cameron is appointed art director for the film *Battle Beyond the Stars.*

1981 Cameron directs his first film, *Piranha II: The Spawning*, which turns out to be a disaster.

2000 Cameron marries fifth wife, Suzy Amis, on June 4.

2001 Cameron and wife Amis welcome the birth of twins, Quinn and Claire, on April 4.

2003 Cameron's documentary *Ghosts of the Abyss* is released.

2005 *Aliens of the Deep*, the follow-up to *Ghosts of the Abyss*, is released.

2006 Daughter Elizabeth Rose is born to Cameron and Amis on December 29.

2009 *Avatar* hits the big screen in December, breaking Cameron's own record for highest-grossing film.

Glossary

analyze
> To examine in detail.

aristocracy
> A class of people possessing exceptional rank, wealth, and privilege.

colonize
> To make or establish a colony upon settling a region.

communism
> A societal theory in which private property is eliminated, and goods are owned together by all.

cyborg
> "cybernetic organism;" a being with both biological and artificial parts.

exoskeleton
> An artificial external-supporting structure.

holocaust
> A massive slaughter of people.

indigenous
> Living or occurring naturally in a particular environment.

microprocessor
> A small computer processor on a microchip.

promenade
> An area on the deck of a passenger ship for strolling, usually reserved for the upper-class passengers.

semiconductor
Electric conductors used in the making of computers.

social norm
Behavioral expectations within a society or group.

socialism
A political theory in which there is no private property, but rather the government owns and controls goods and materials and the production and distribution of them.

steerage
Inferior accommodations on a passenger ship for those paying the lowest fares.

stereotype
A traditional concept or type.

submersible
A small underwater craft used in deep-sea research.

surrogate
One who takes the place of another as a substitute.

tenet
A belief or doctrine generally accepted as truth.

Bibliography of Works and Criticism

Important Works

Piranha II: The Spawning, 1981

The Terminator, 1984

Rambo: First Blood Part II, 1985

Aliens, 1986

The Abyss, 1989

Terminator 2: Judgment Day, 1991

True Lies, 1994

Titanic, 1997

Dark Angel, 2000–2003

Ghosts of the Abyss, 2003

Aliens of the Deep, 2005

Terminator: The Sarah Connor Chronicles, 2008–2009

Avatar, 2009

Critical Discussions

Braudy, Leo, and Marshall Cohen, eds. *Film Theory and Criticism: Introductory Readings*. New York: Oxford UP, 2009. Print.

Keller, Alexandra. *James Cameron*. New York: Routledge, 2006. Print.

Monaco, James. *How to Read a Film: Movies, Media and Beyond: Art, Technology, Language, History, Theory*. New York: Oxford UP, 2009. Print.

Resources

Selected Bibliography

Aliens. Dir. James Cameron. Twentieth Century Fox, 1986. DVD.

Avatar. Dir. James Cameron. Twentieth Century Fox, 2009. DVD.

Keegan, Rebecca. *The Futurist: The Life and Films of James Cameron*. New York: Random House, 2009. Print.

The Terminator. Dir. James Cameron. Orion Pictures, 1984. DVD.

Titanic. Dir. James Cameron. Twentieth Century Fox, 1997. DVD.

Further Readings

Parisi, Paula. *Titanic and the Making of James Cameron: The Inside Story of the Three-Year Adventure That Rewrote Motion Picture History*. New York: Newmarket, 1998. Print.

Wilshin, Mark. *A Cinematic History of Sci-Fi & Fantasy*. Chicago: Raintree, 2005.

Wolf, Steve. *The Secret Science Behind Movie Stunts and Special Effects*. New York: Skyhorse, 2008. Print.

Yasuda, Anita. *James Cameron*. New York: AV2, 2010. Print.

Web Links

To learn more about critiquing the films of James Cameron, visit ABDO Publishing Company online at **www.abdopublishing.com**. Web sites about the films of James Cameron are featured on our Book Links page. These links are routinely monitored and updated to provide the most current information available.

For More Information

The Academy of Motion Picture Arts and Sciences
8949 Wilshire Boulevard, Beverly Hills, CA 990211
310-247-3000
www.oscars.org

The Academy holds many exhibitions, movie screenings, lectures, and other events related to the film industry.

San Francisco Film Museum
1755 Van Ness Avenue, Suite 101, San Francisco, CA 94109
415-652-0249
sanfranciscofilmmuseum.org

The San Francisco Film Museum examines the history of filmmaking.

Source Notes

Chapter 1. Introduction to Critiques
None.

Chapter 2. A Closer Look at James Cameron
1. Rebecca Keegan. *The Futurist: The Life and Films of James Cameron*. New York: Random House, 2009. Print. 11.
2. Ibid.

Chapter 3. An Overview of *The Terminator*
1. *The Terminator*. Dir. James Cameron. Orion Pictures, 1984. DVD.
2. Ibid.
3. Ibid.
4. Ibid.
5. Ibid.

Chapter 4. How to Apply Historical Criticism to *The Terminator*

1. Moira Johnston. "High Tech, High Risk and High Life in Silicon Valley." *National Geographic*. Volume 162, No. 4 (October 1982): 463.

2. Jay David Bolter. *Turing's Man: Western Culture in the Computer Age*. University of North Carolina, 1984. 3-4.

3. *The Terminator*. Dir. James Cameron. Orion Pictures, 1984. DVD.

Chapter 5. An Overview of *Aliens*

1. *Aliens*. Dir. James Cameron. Twentieth Century Fox, 1986. DVD.

2. Ibid.

3. Ibid.

Chapter 6. How to Apply Feminist Criticism to *Aliens*

1. *Aliens*. Dir. James Cameron. Twentieth Century Fox, 1986. DVD.

2. Ibid.

3. Ibid.

Source Notes Continued

Chapter 7. An Overview of *Titanic*

None.

Chapter 8. How to Apply Marxist Criticism to *Titanic*

1. *Titanic*. Dir. James Cameron. Twentieth Century Fox, 1997. DVD.

2. Ibid.

3. Ibid.

4. Ibid.

5. Ibid.

6. Ibid.

7. "Private Property and Communism." *Marxists Internet Archive*. n.p., n.d. Web. 5 Oct. 2010.

Chapter 9. An Overview of *Avatar*

1. *Avatar*. Dir. James Cameron. Twentieth Century Fox, 2009. DVD.

2. Ibid.

3. Ibid.

Chapter 10. How to Apply Postcolonial Criticism to *Avatar*

1. Charles E. Bressler. *Literary Criticism: An Introduction to Theory and Practice*. Upper Saddle River, NJ: Prentice Hall, 1994. Print. 203.

2. *Avatar*. Dir. James Cameron. Twentieth Century Fox, 2009. DVD.

3. Ibid.

Index

About the Author

Susan E. Hamen has written educational books on a variety of topics. This is her tenth book. Hamen delights in living amid the changing seasons of her home state, Minnesota, with her family.

Photo Credits

Katy Winn/AP Images, cover, 3; Reed Saxon/AP Images, 12, 98; Matt Sayles/AP Images, 19, 99; Orion Pictures/ Photofest, 20, 28, 32; 20th Century Fox/Photofest, 38, 46, 51, 81; Twentieth Century Fox/Photofest, 58; Paramount Pictures/Photofest, 63; Douglas Kirkland/Paramount Pictures/ Photofest, 66; Paramount Pictures/Photofest, 71; Twentieth Century-Fox Film Corporation /Photofest, 78, 86, 92